Soothing Mandala
Adult Relaxation

Coloring Book

Sans Sargent

www.glendowermedia.com

Glendower Media
Whitmore Lake, Michigan 48189

ISBN

Introduction

Release yourself from the tension of the day and surrender to the soft, easy world of swirling color that you create. Rest and recharge as you create things of beauty, sensuality and wealth.

We recommend colored pencils or markers to bring out true colors and hues for your pictures. There will be no bleed thru so your pictures will retain their basic tones just as you placed them on the page.

Coloring is fun, relaxing and stress free.

And we all need that in our lives.

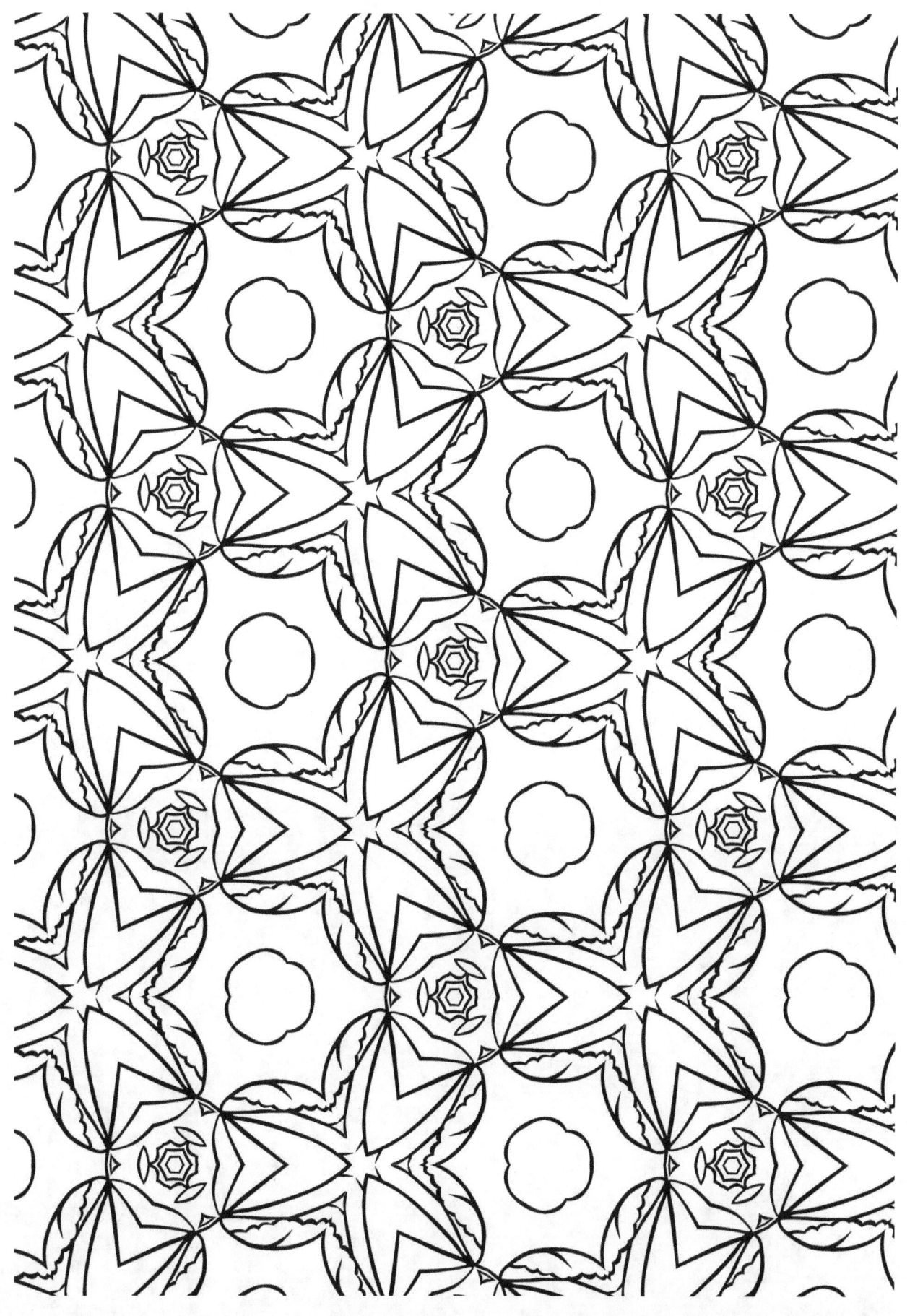

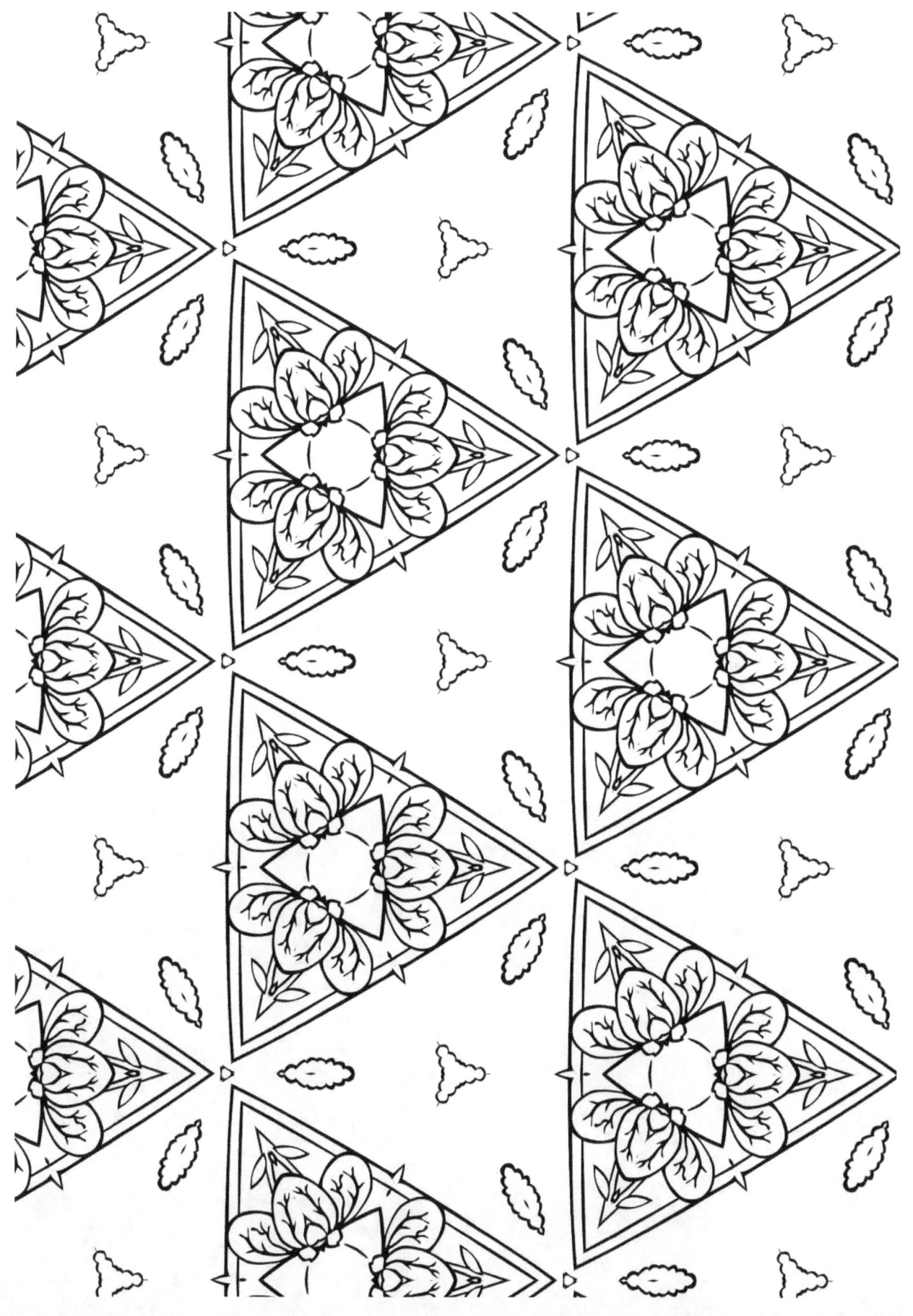

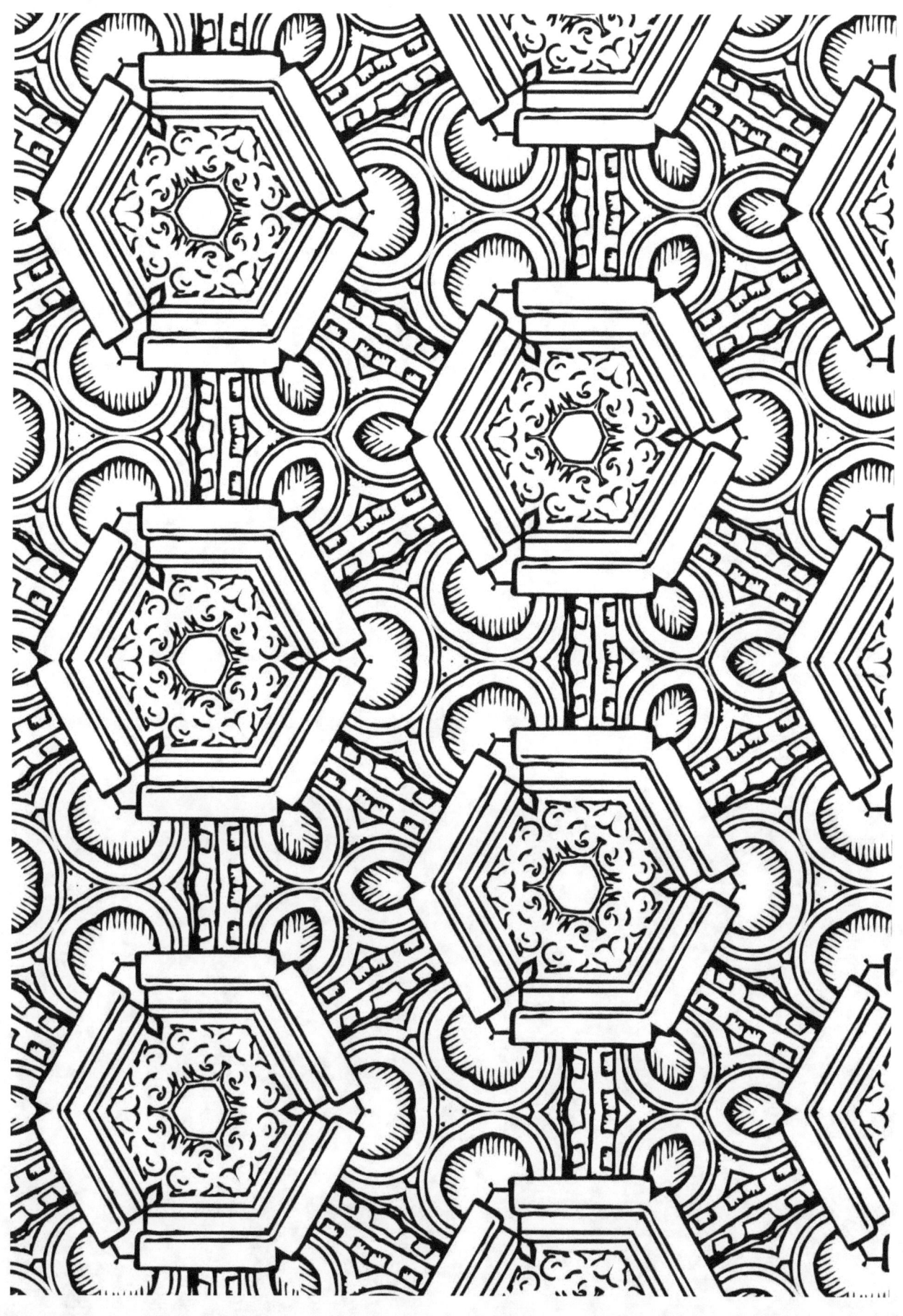

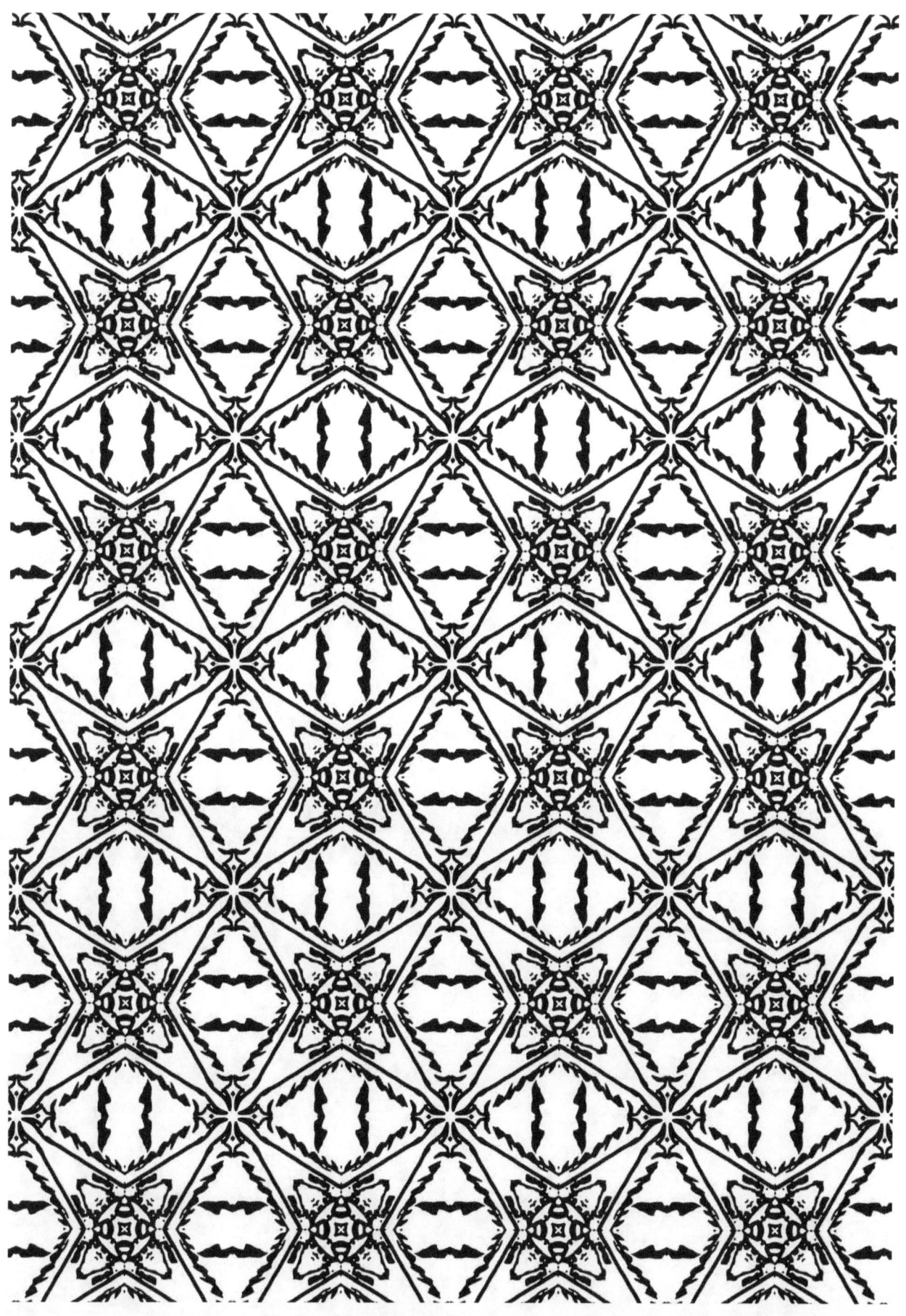

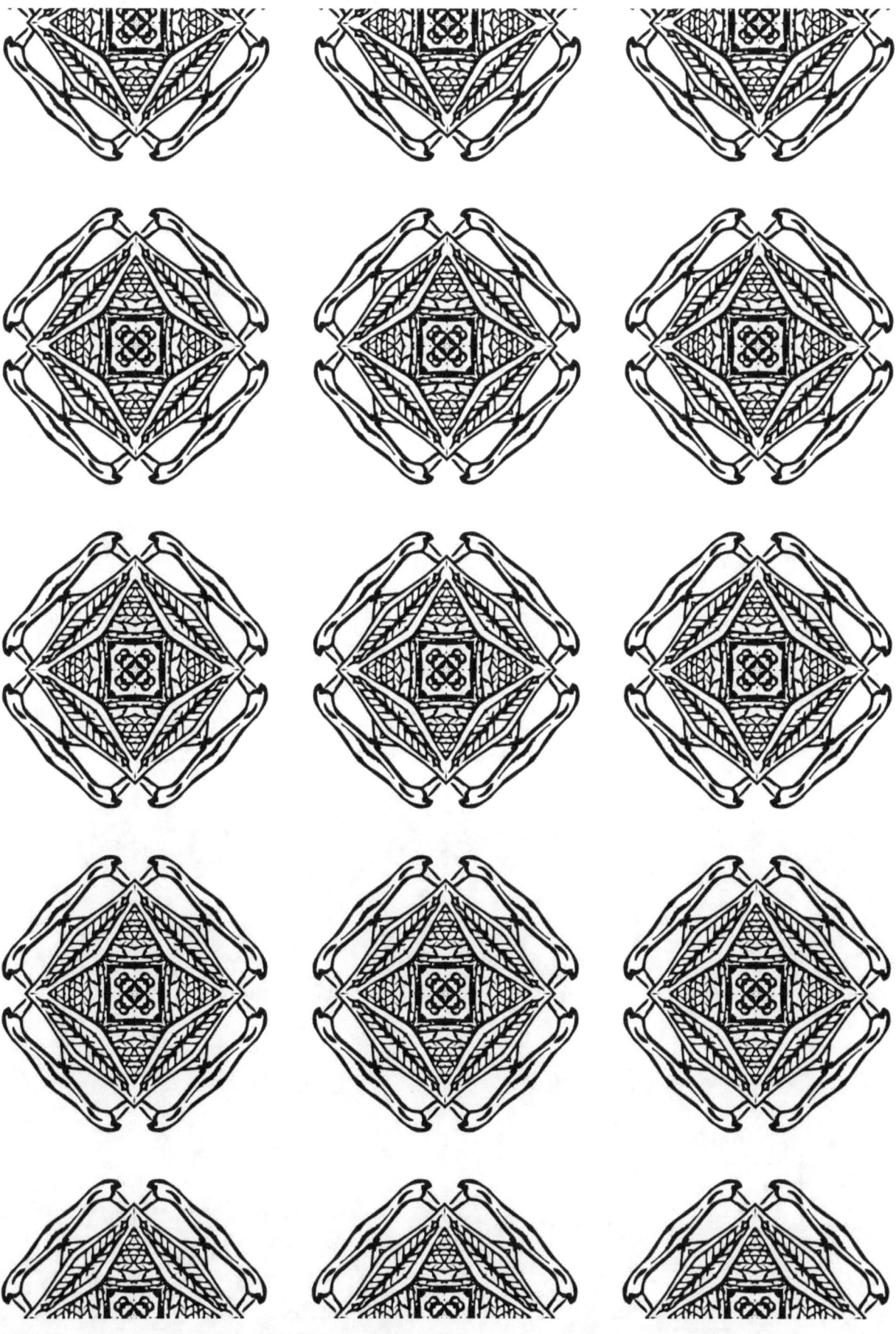

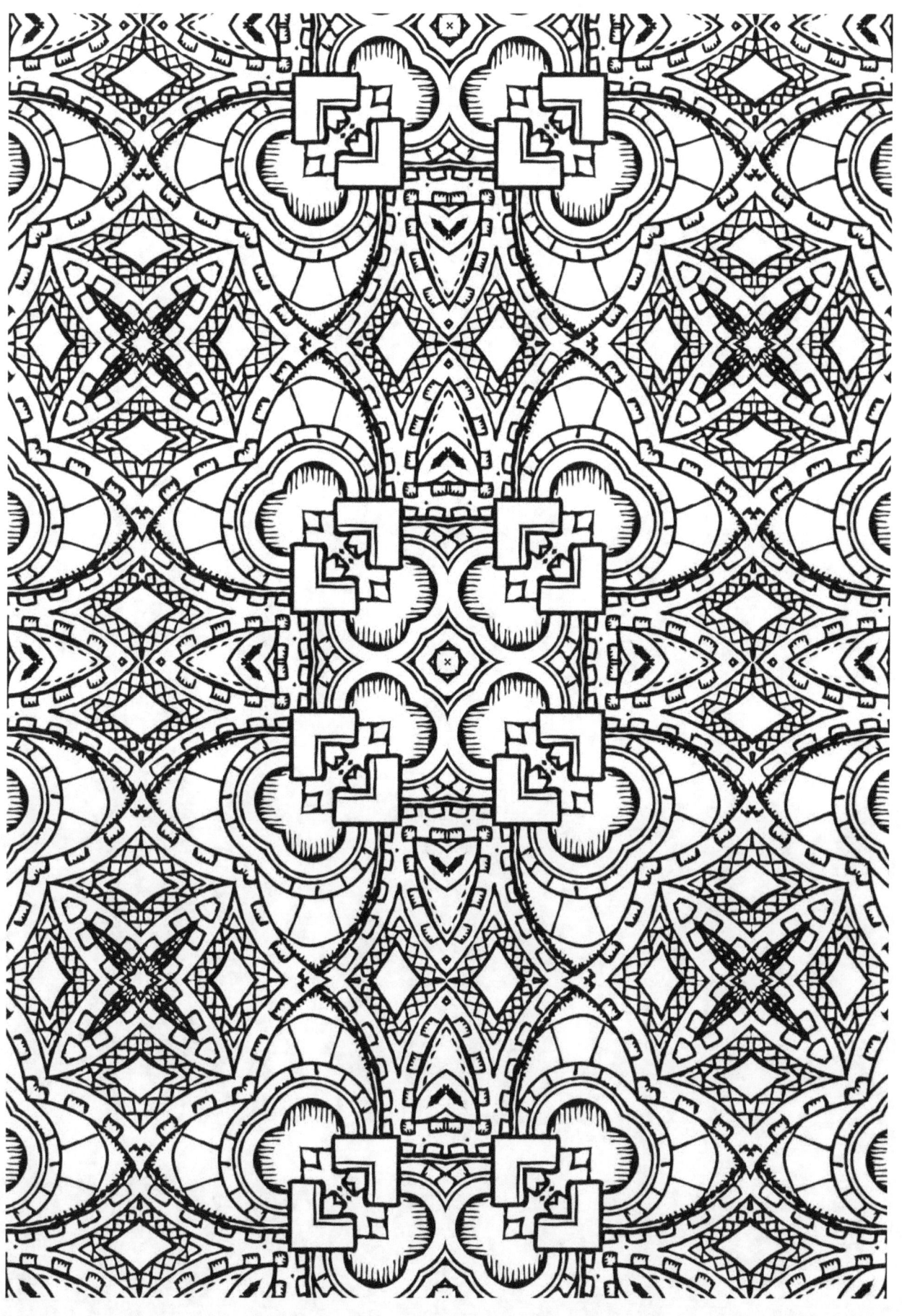

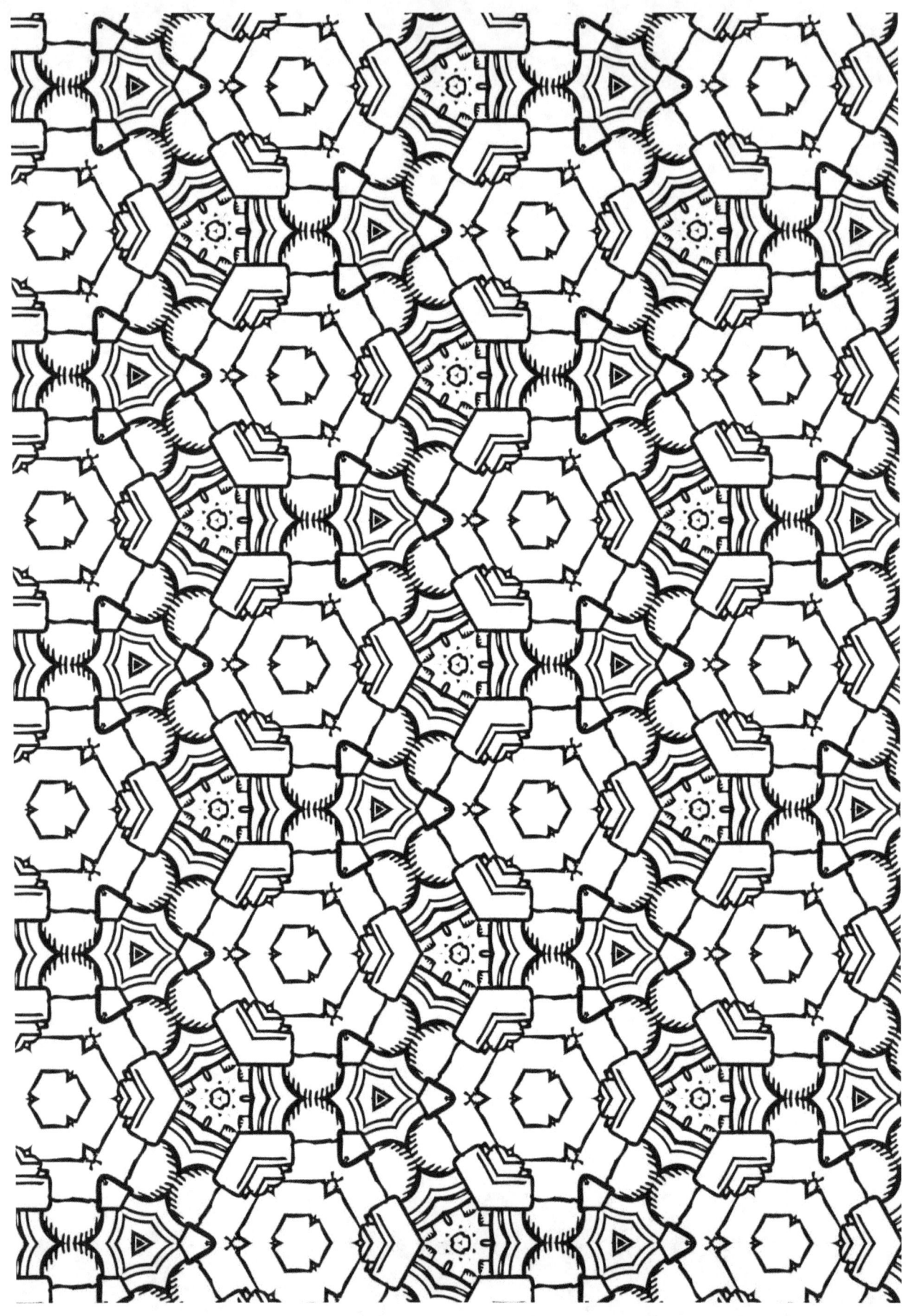

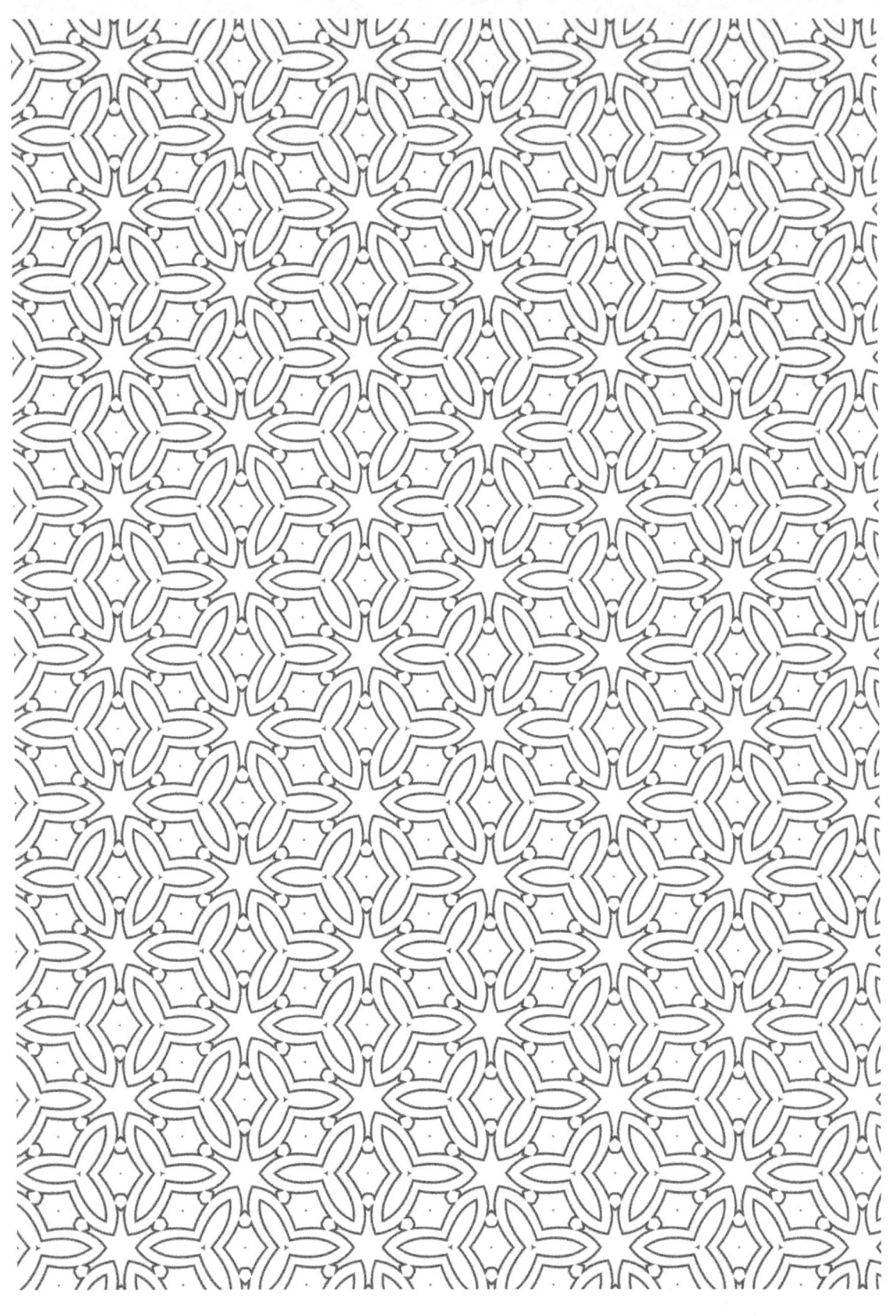

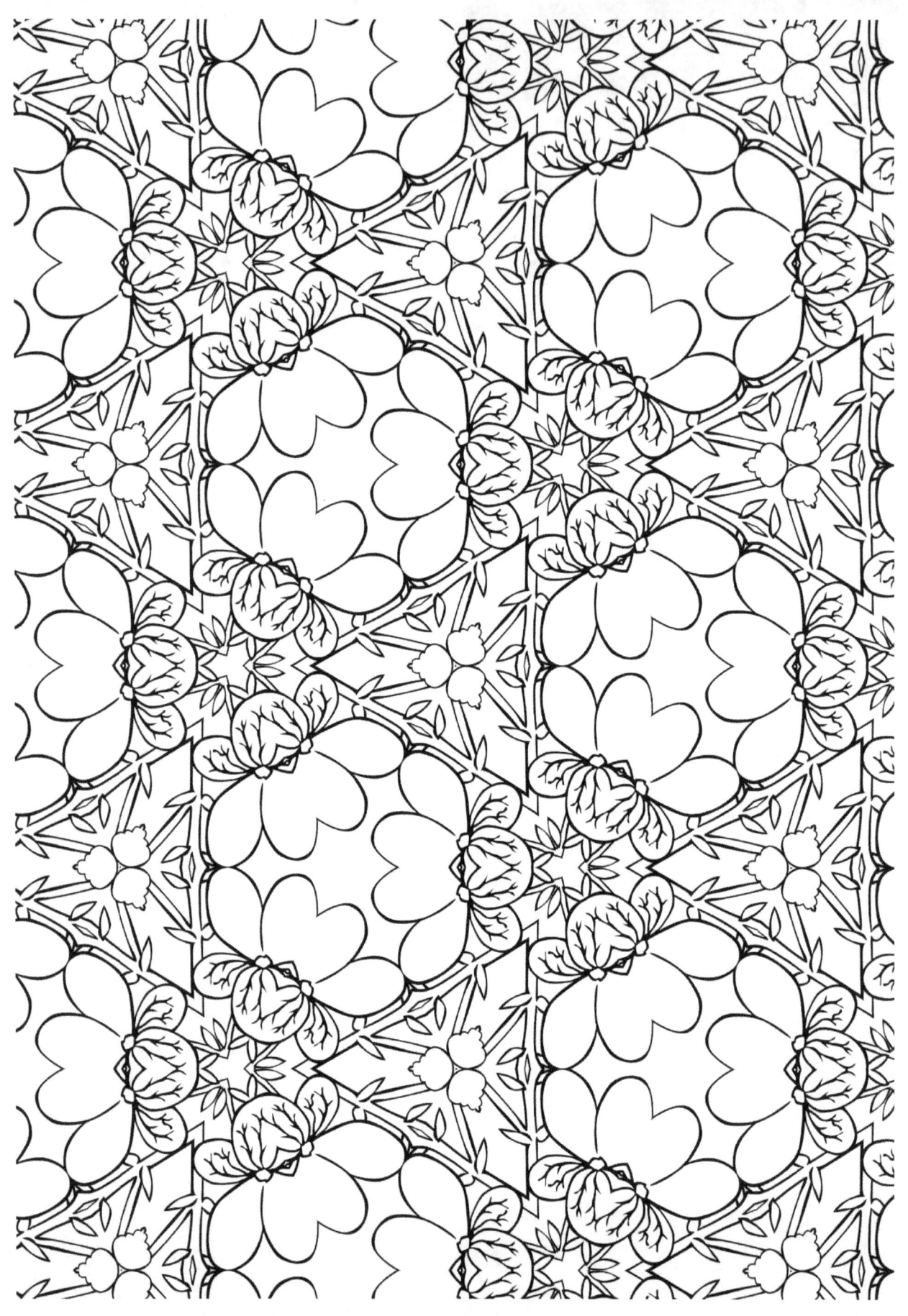

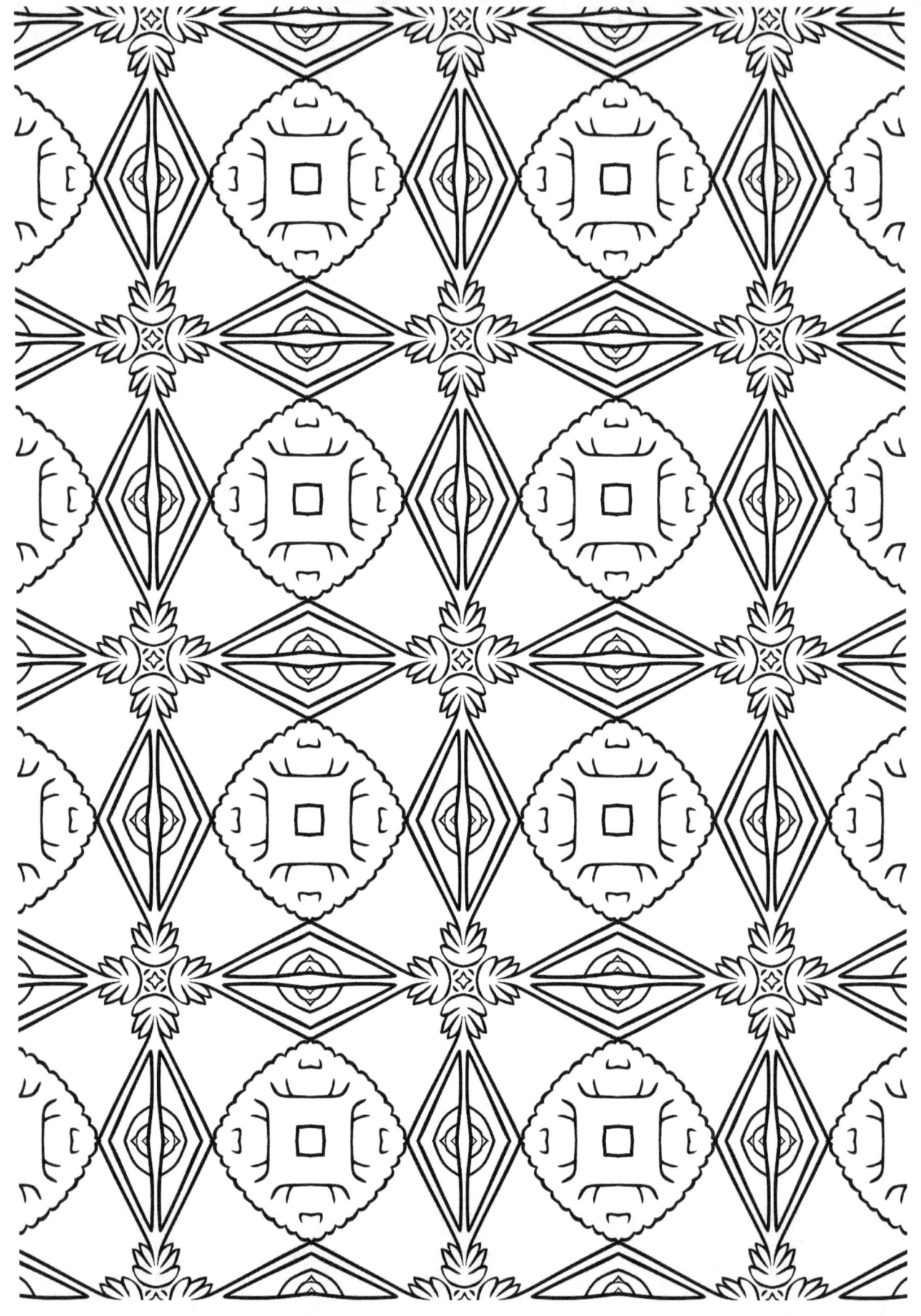

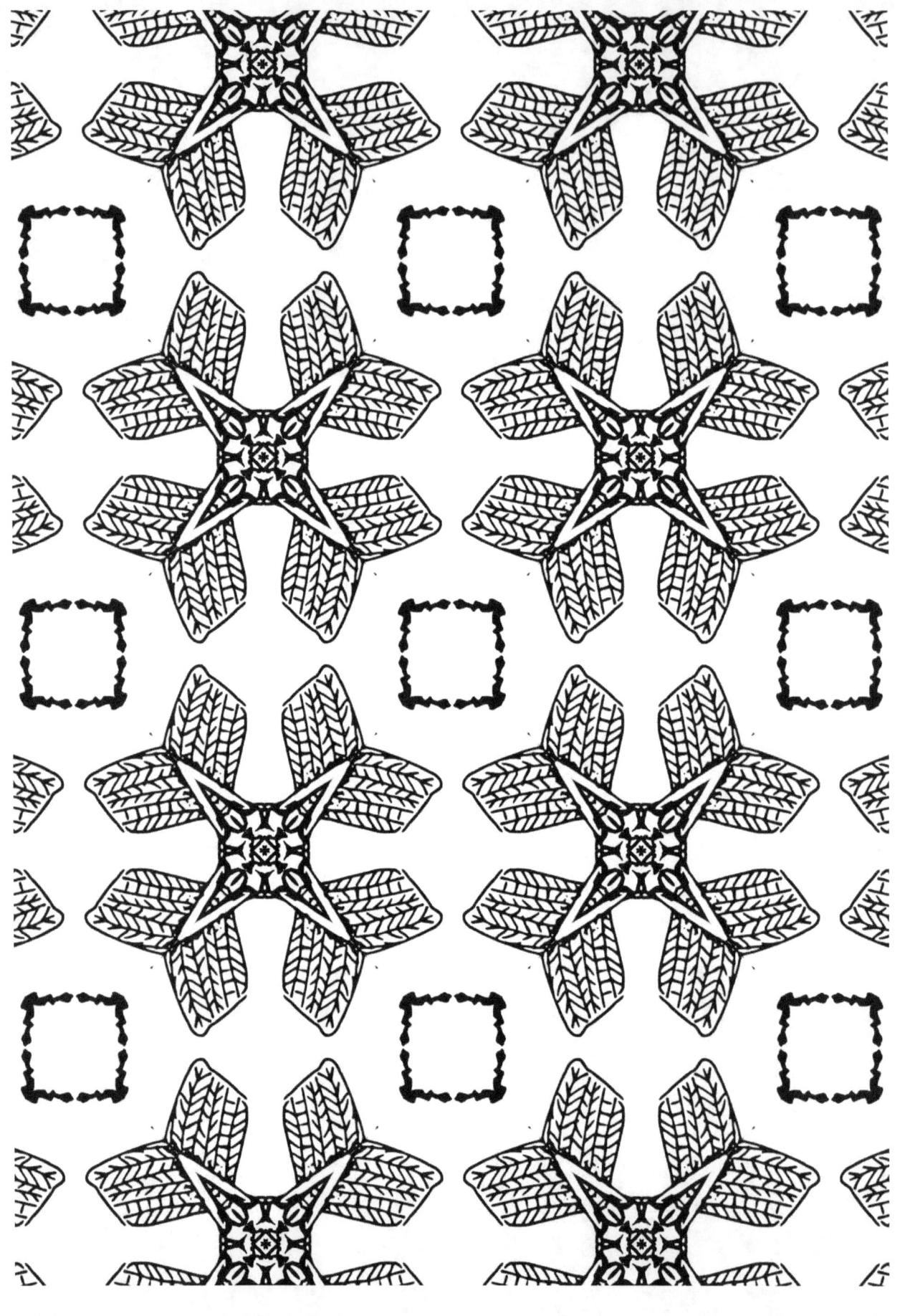

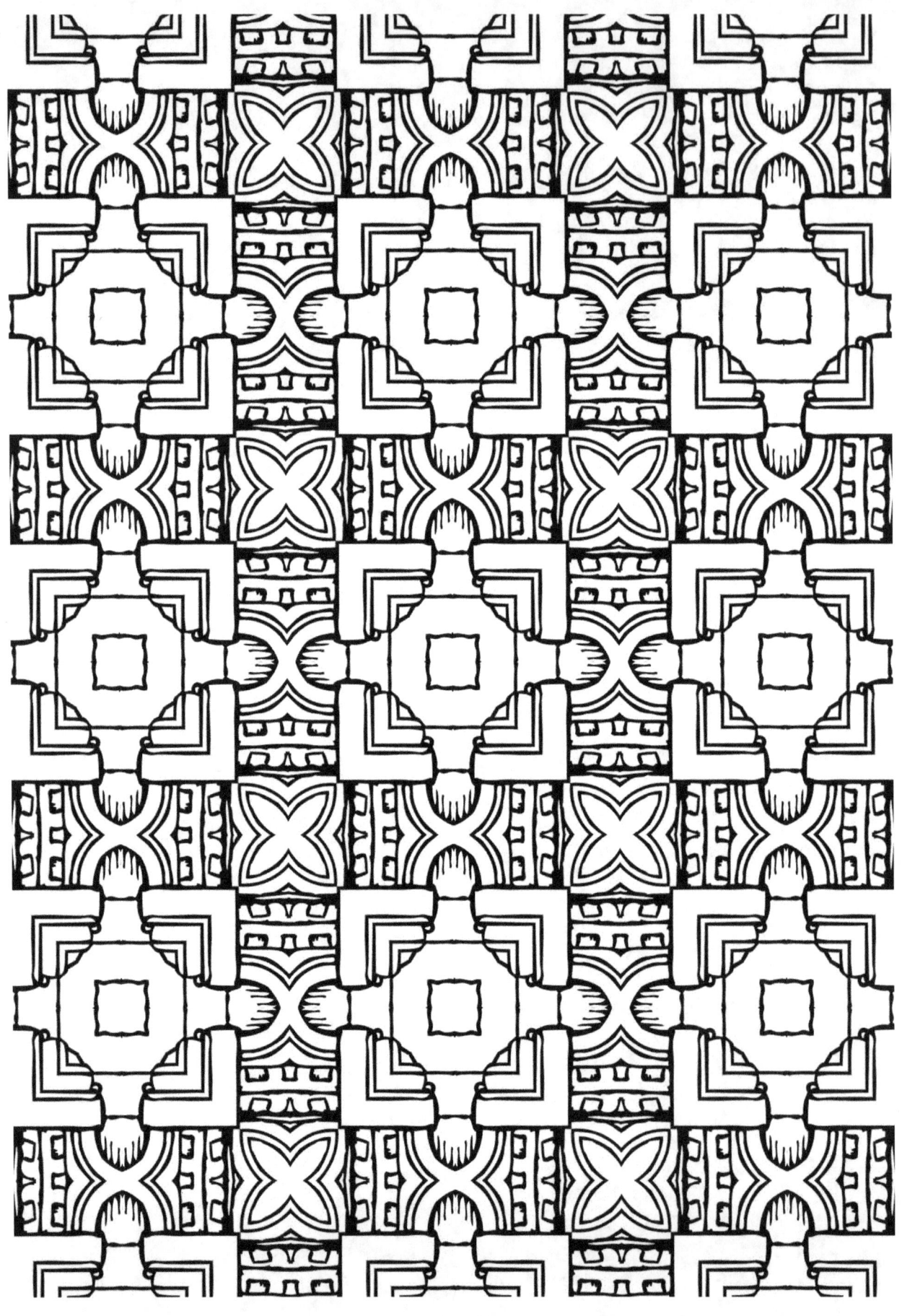

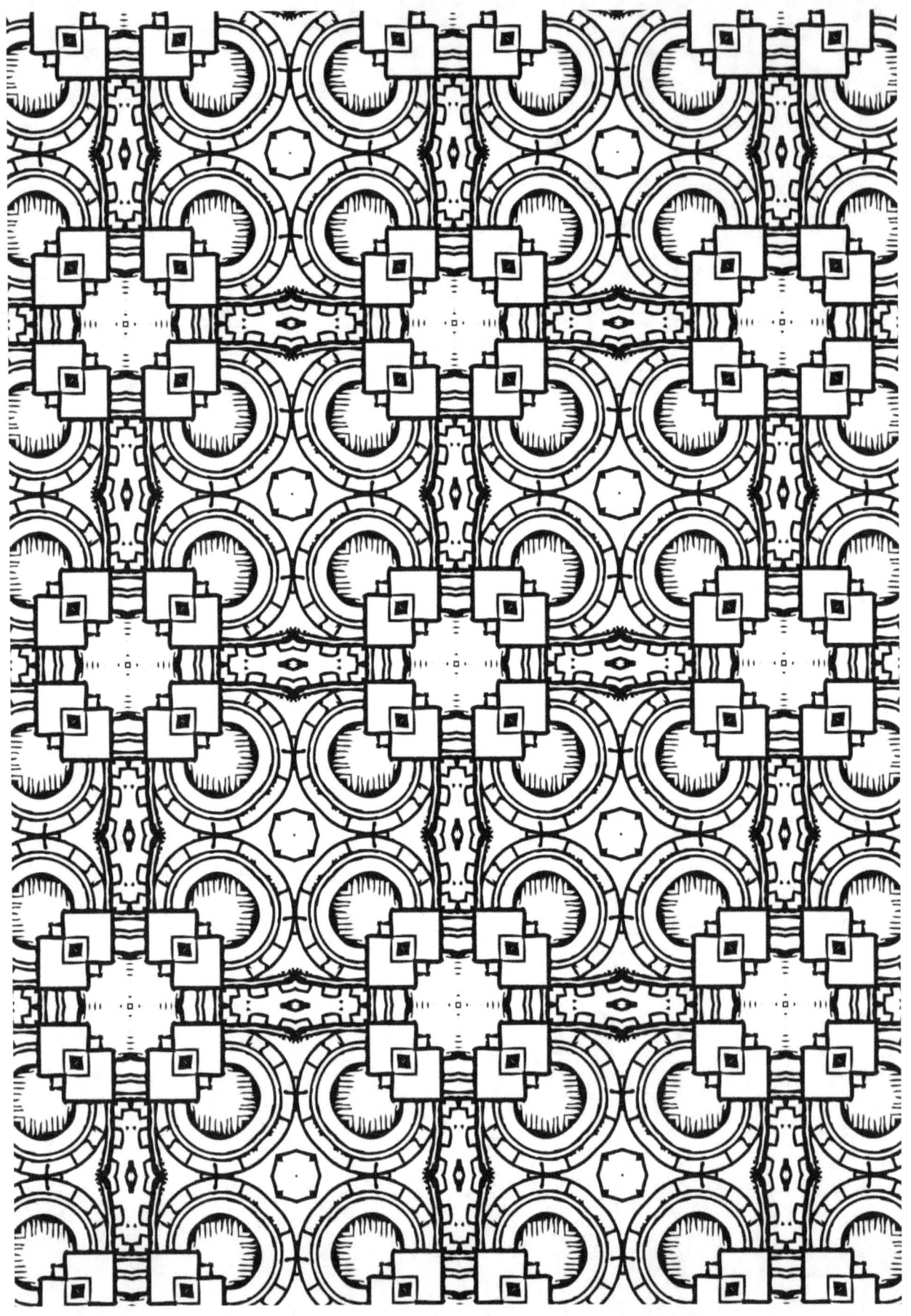

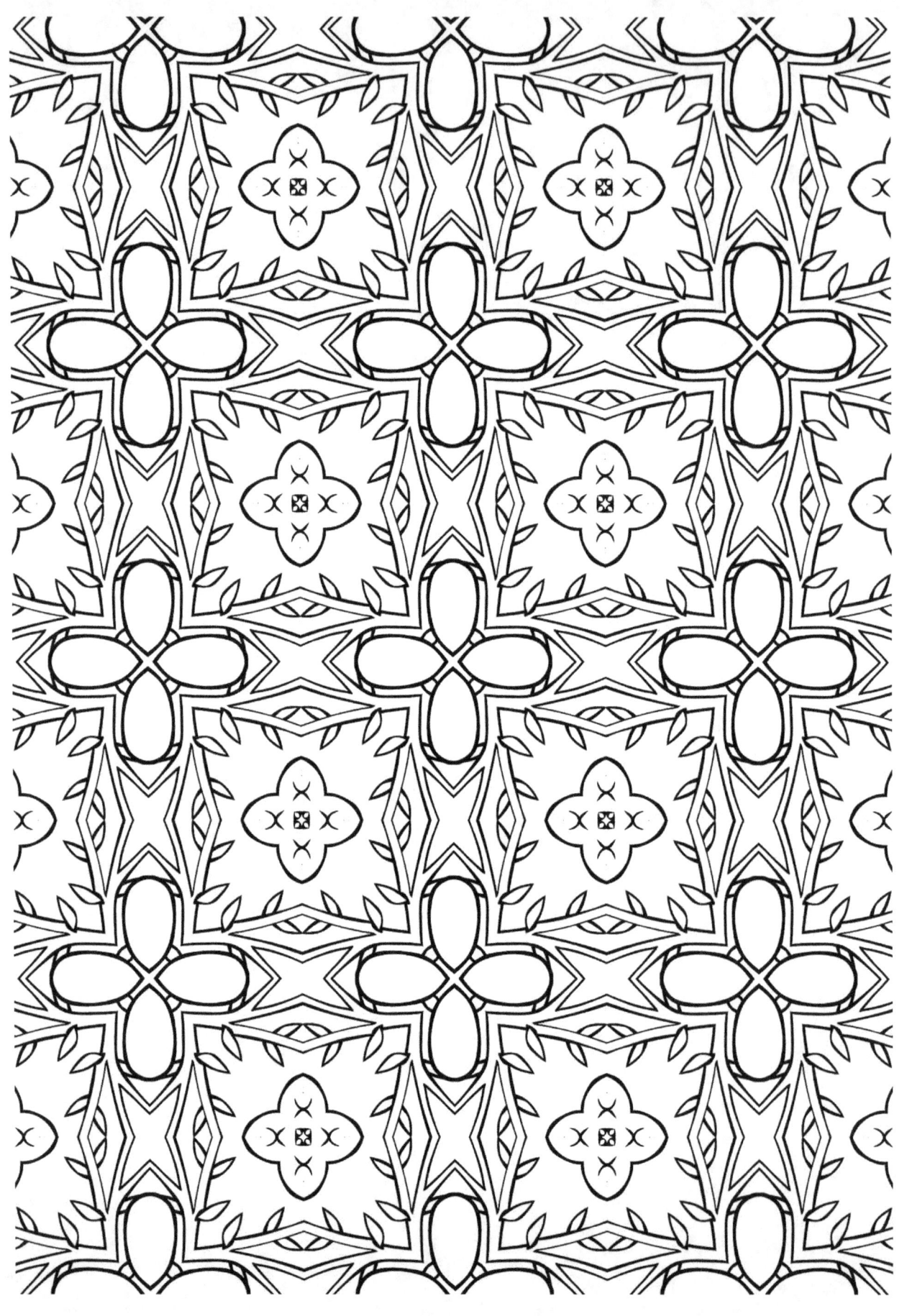

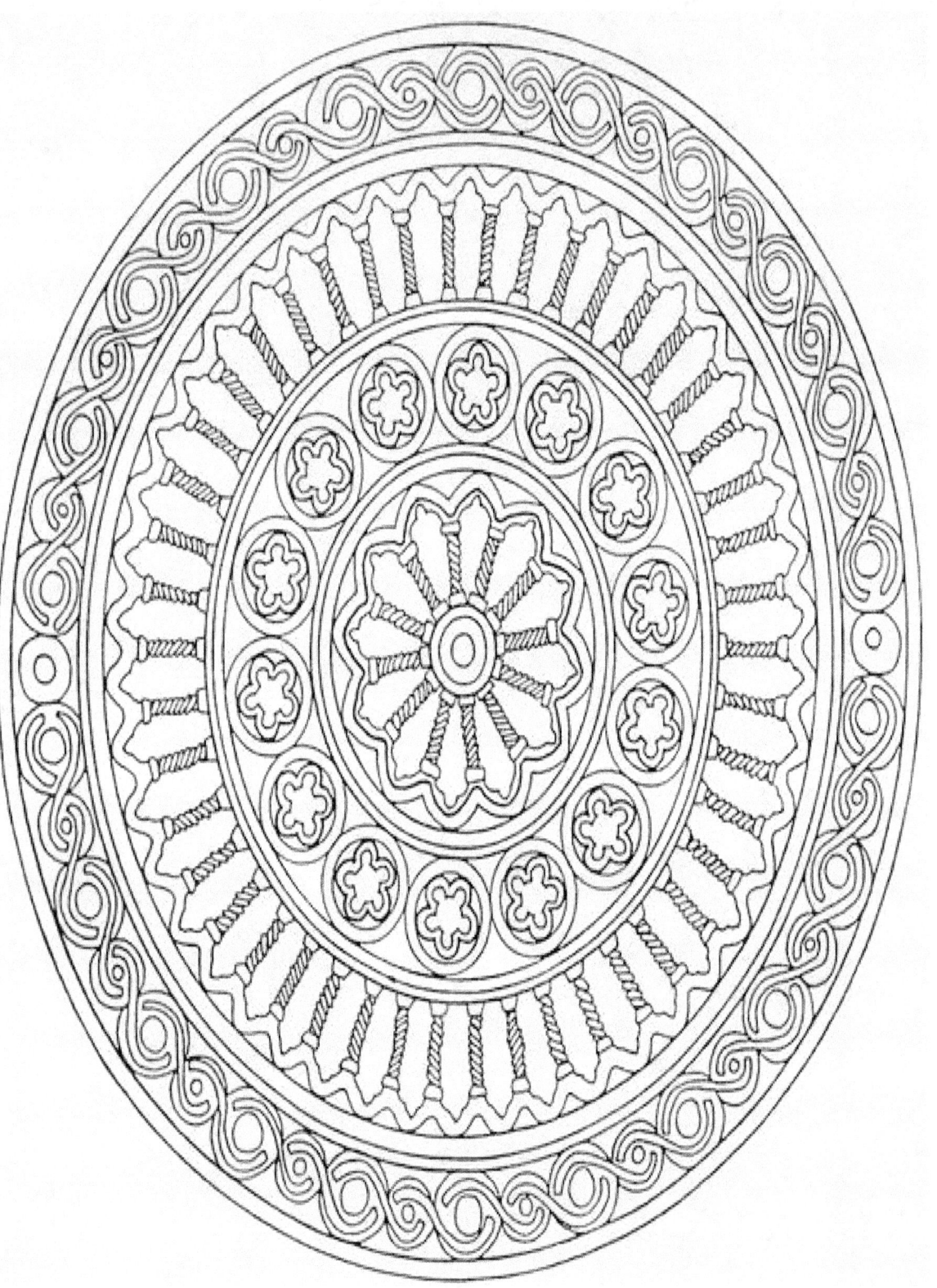

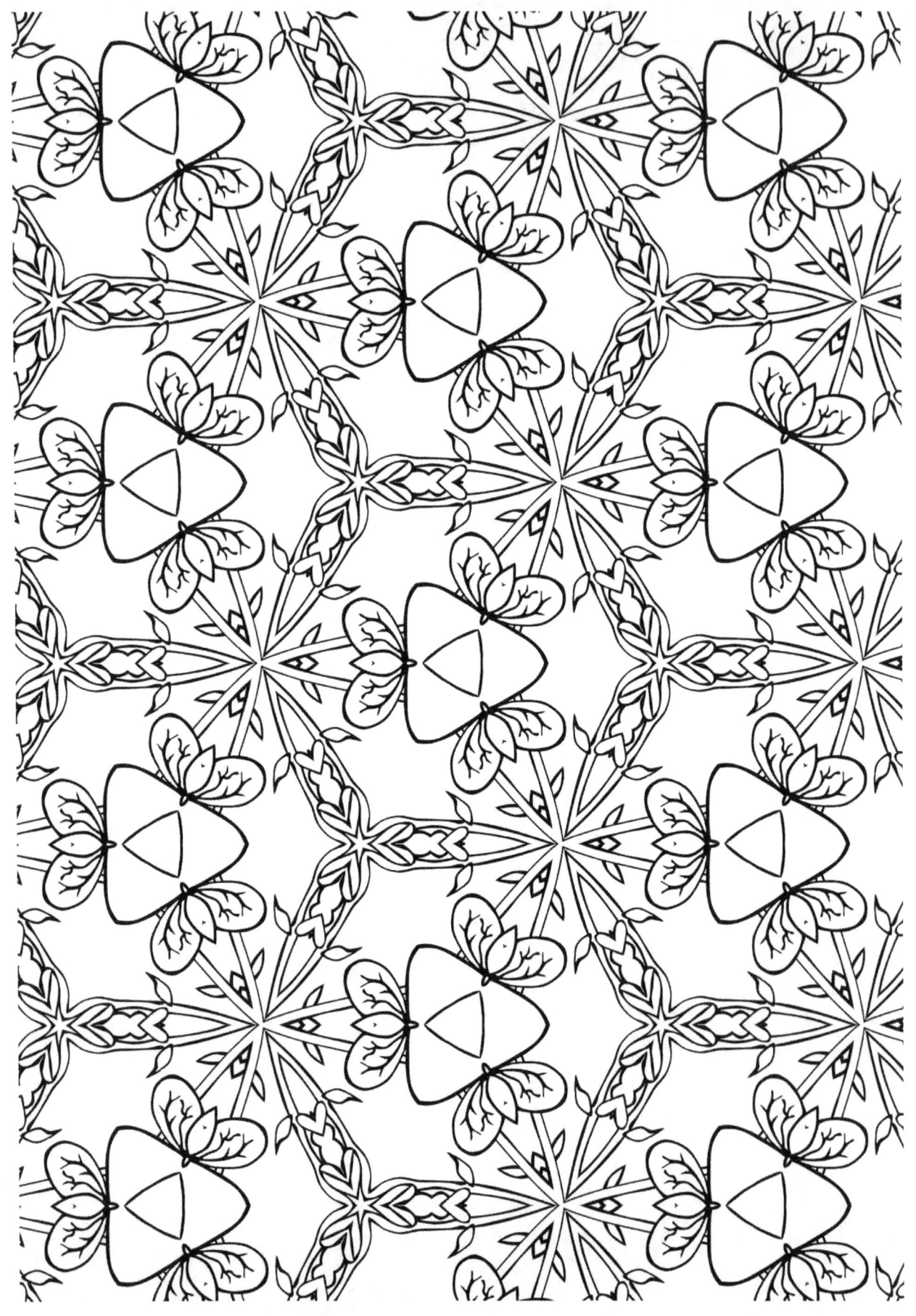

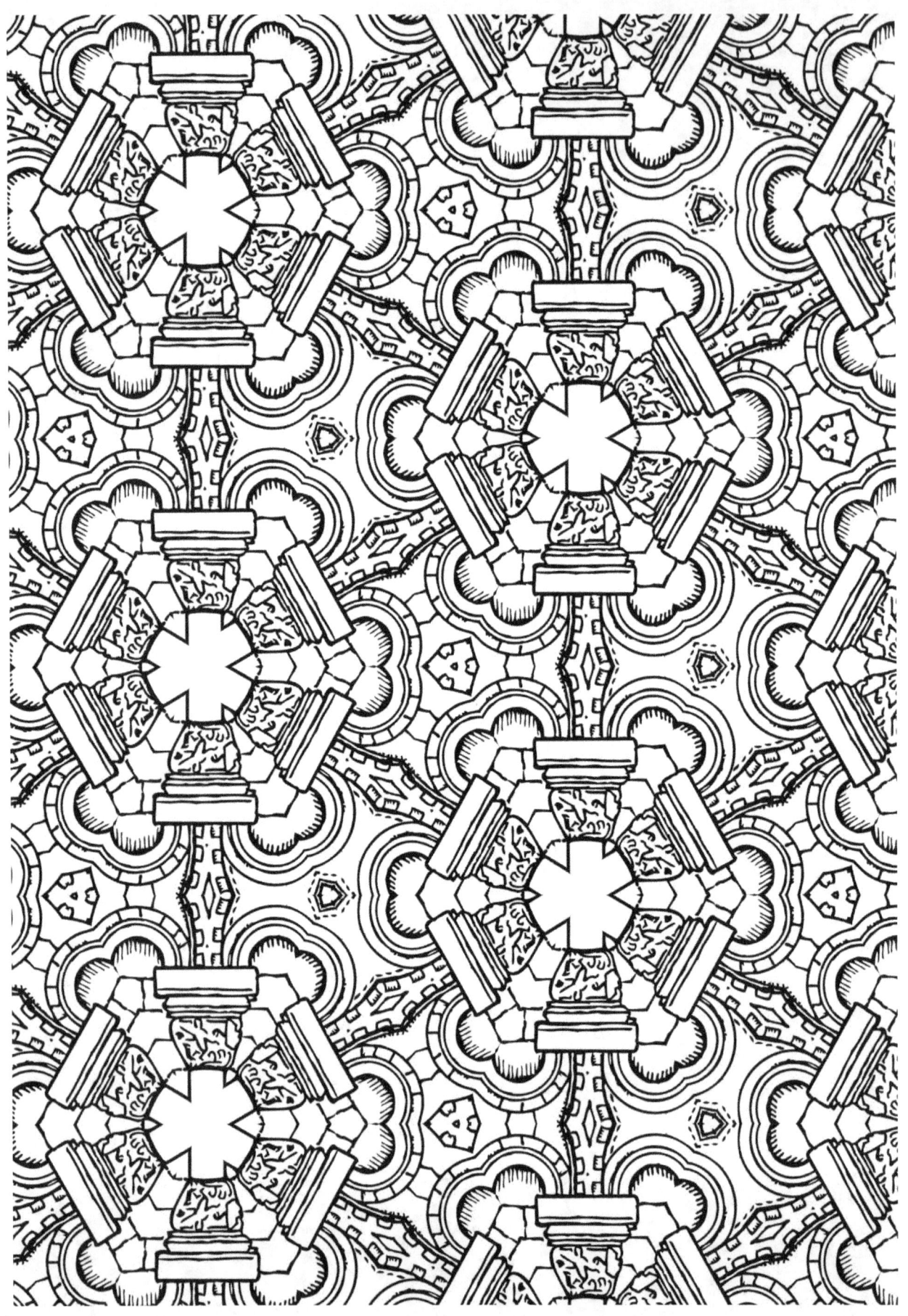

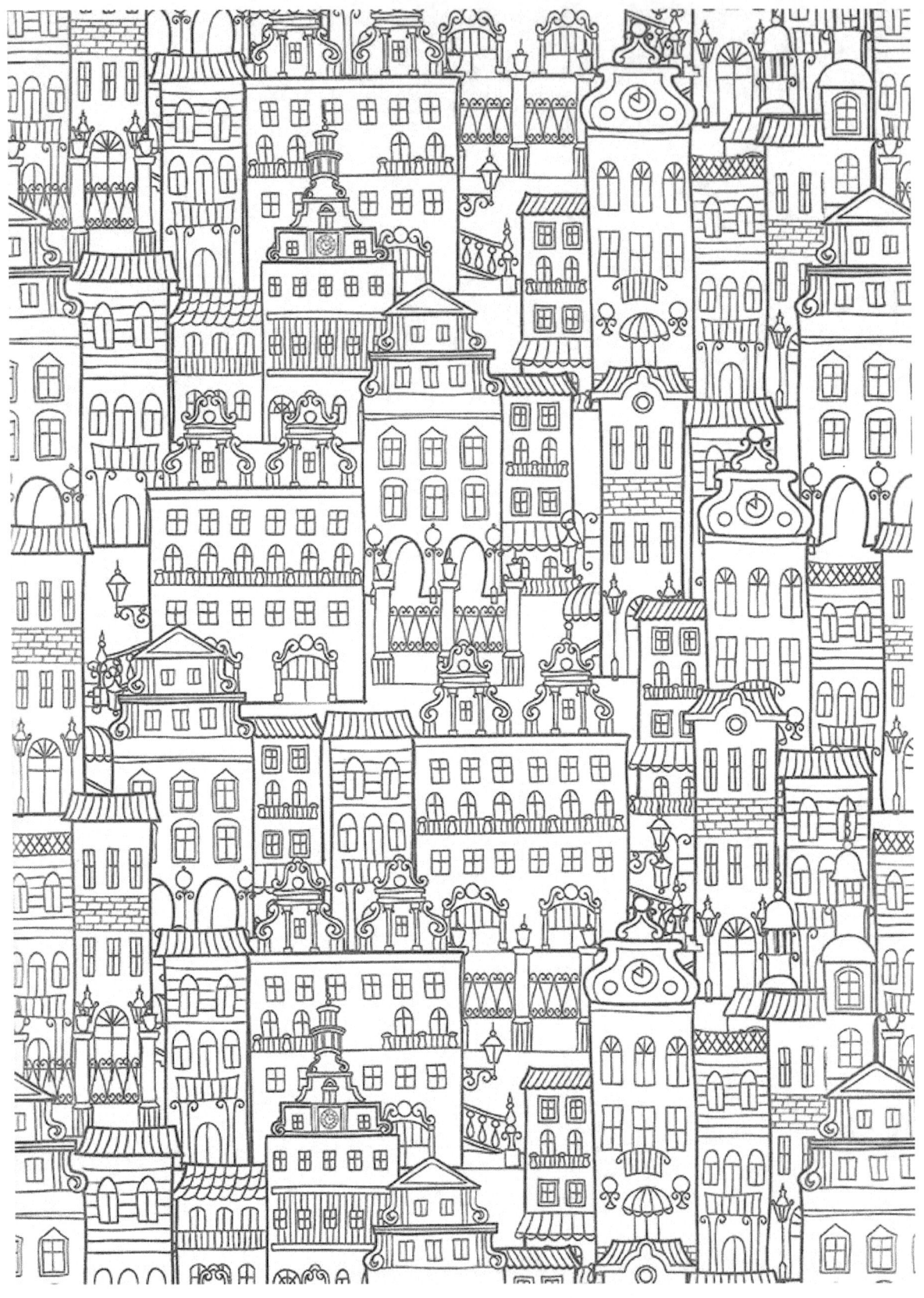

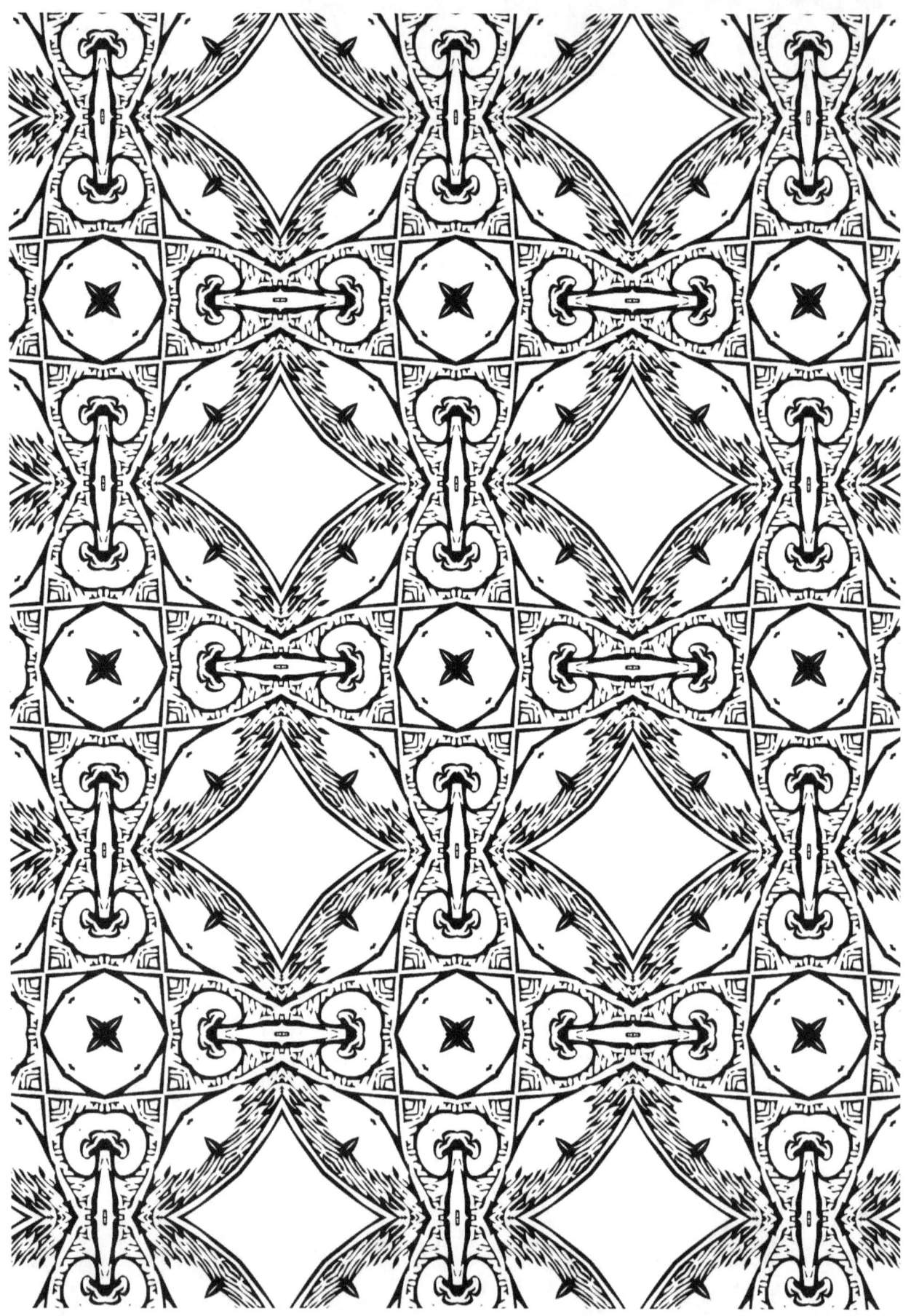

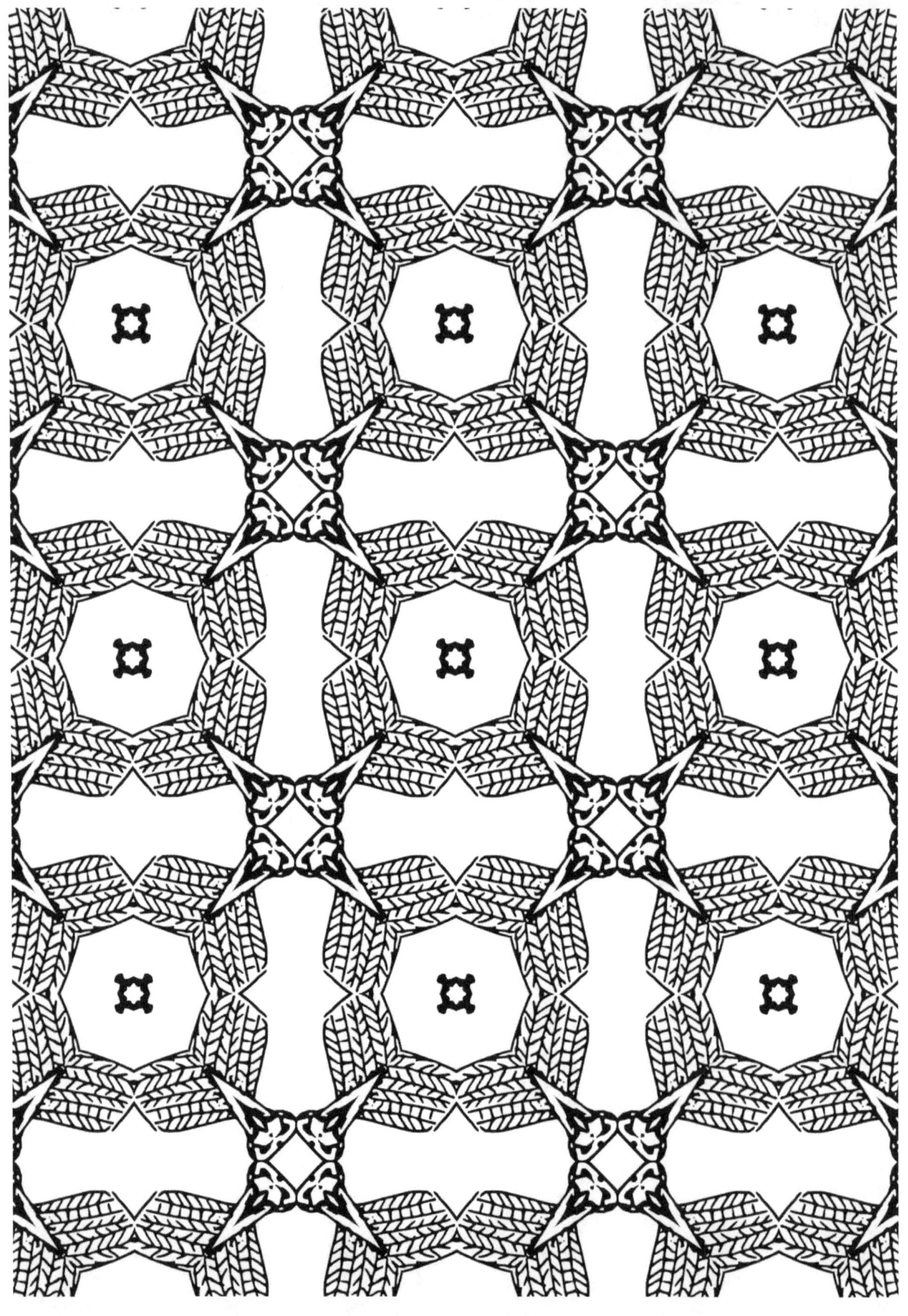

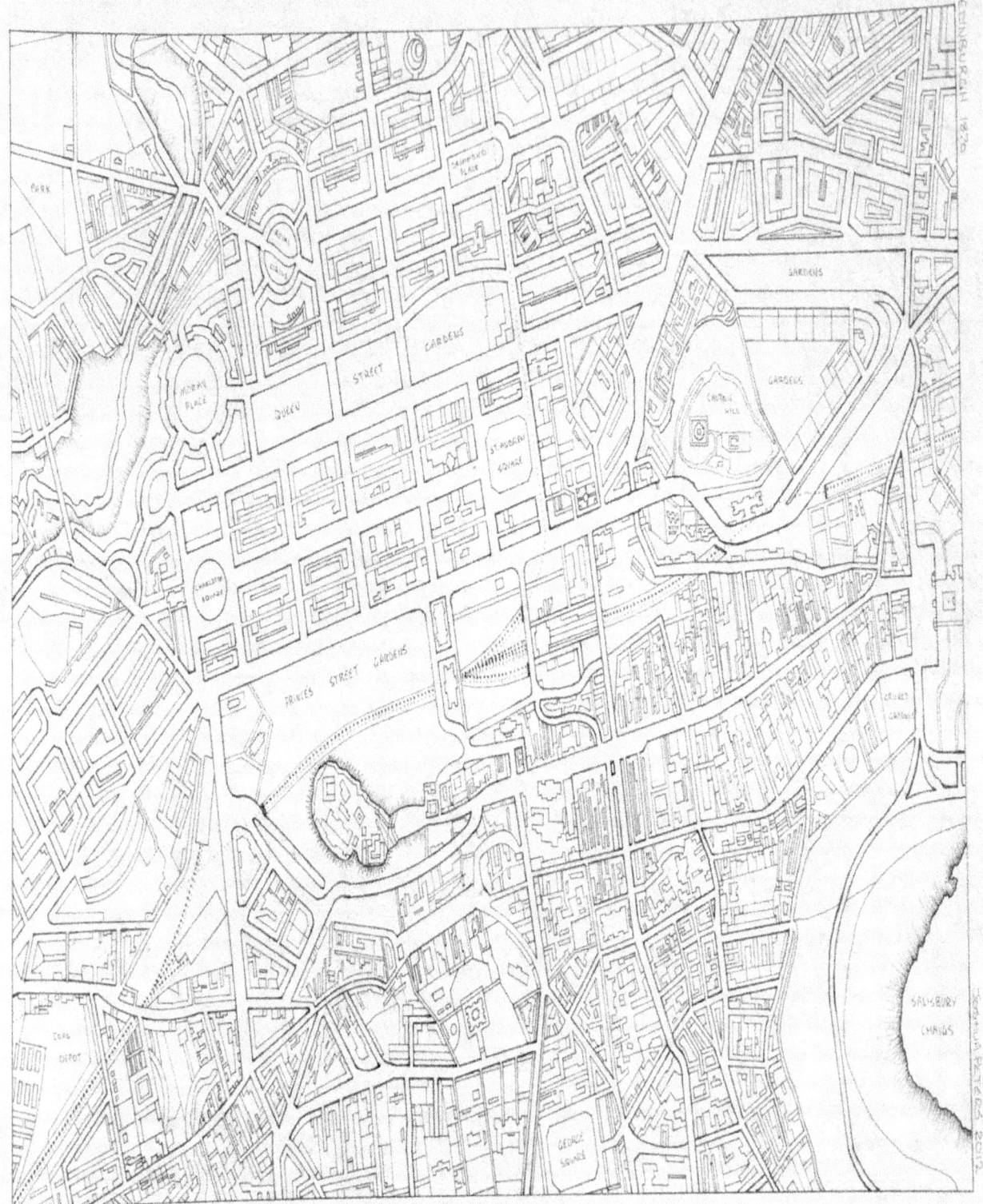

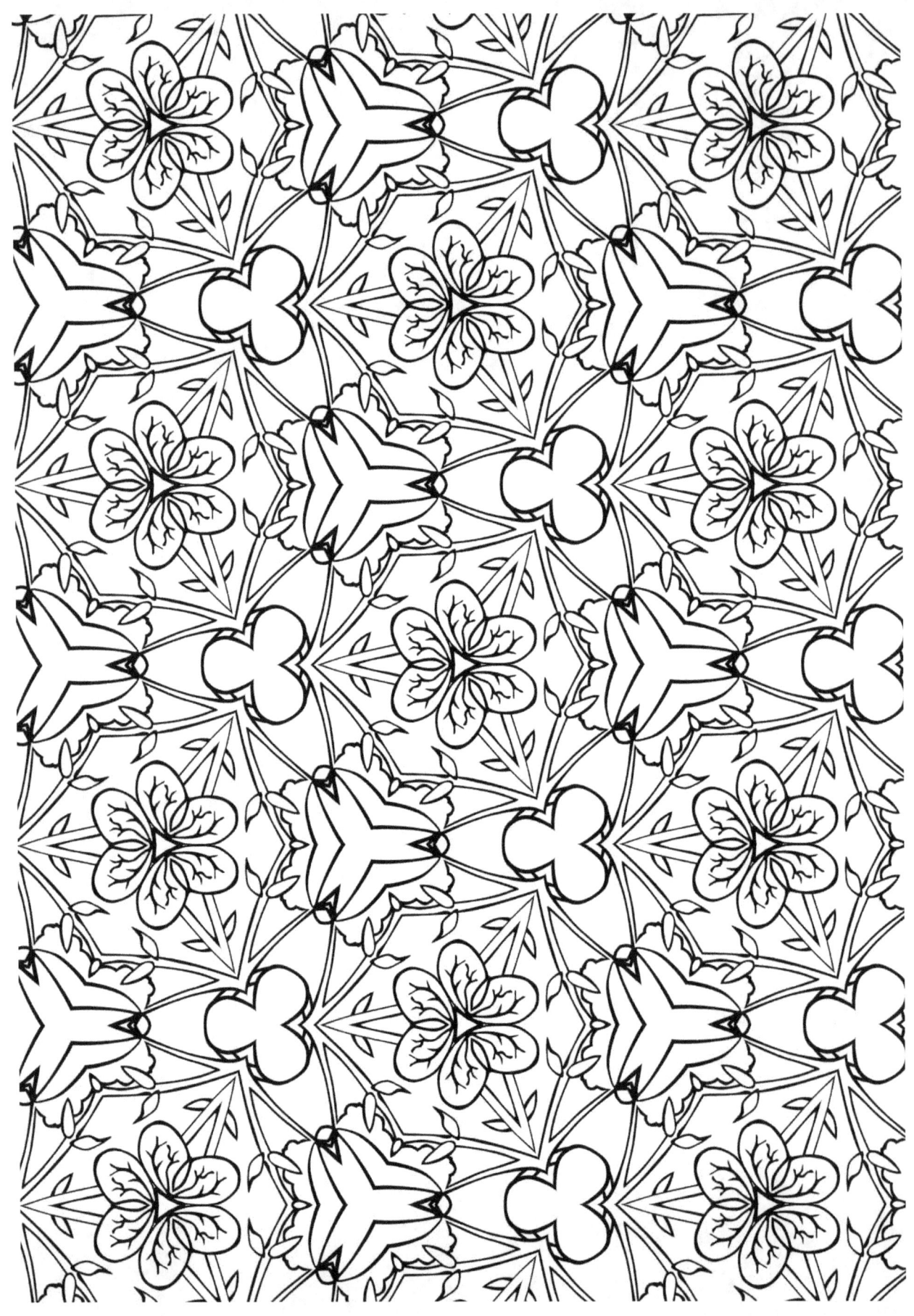

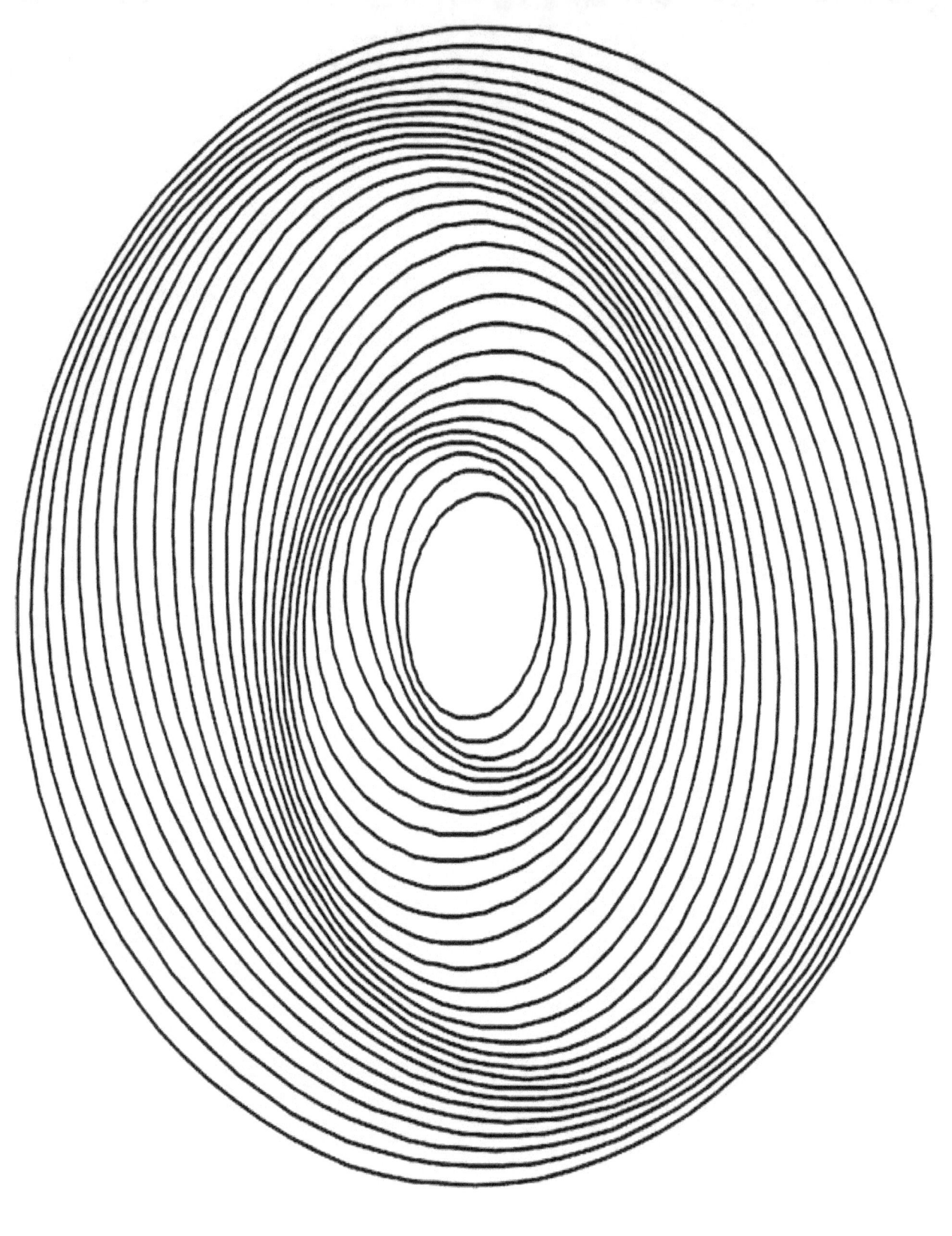

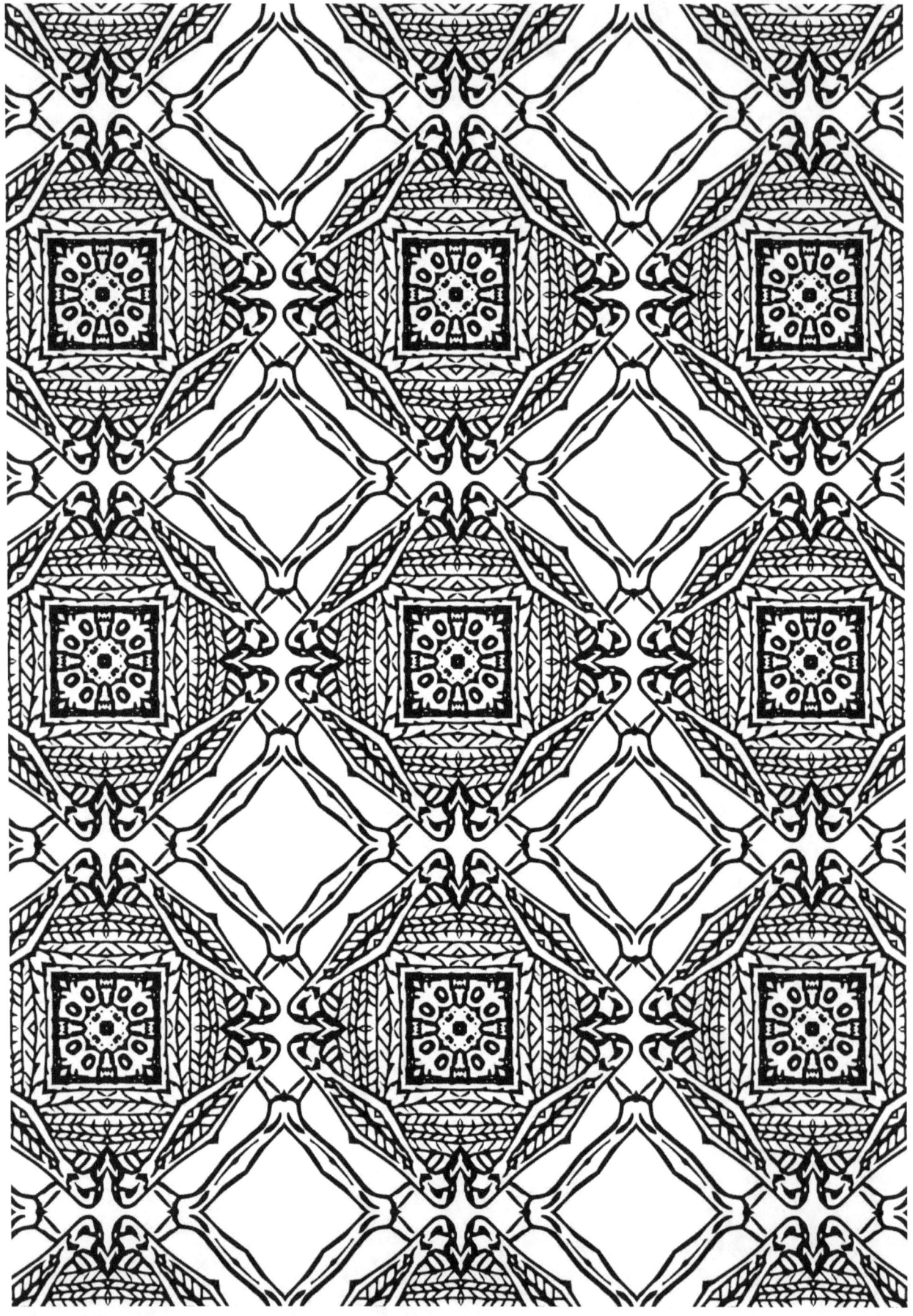

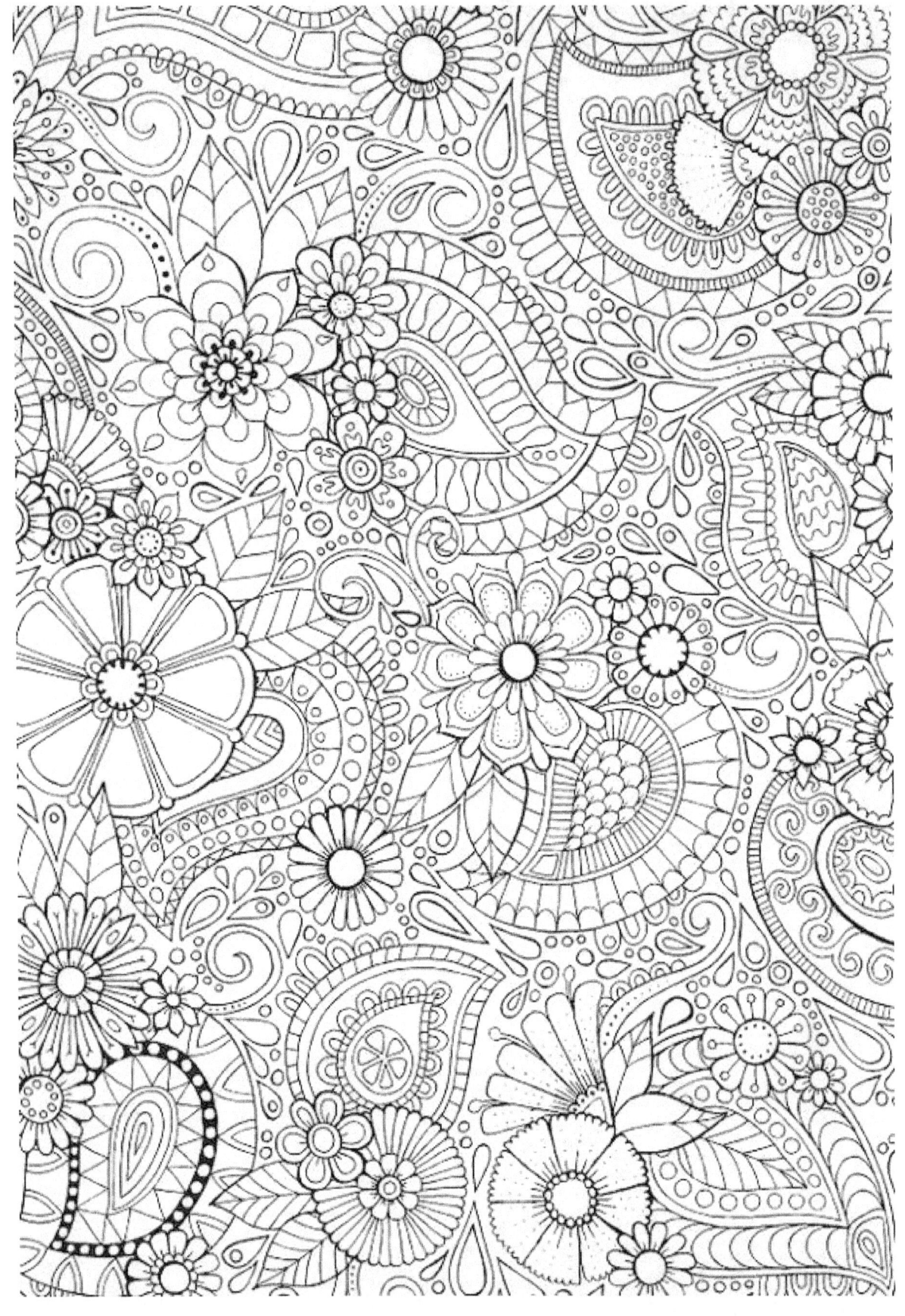

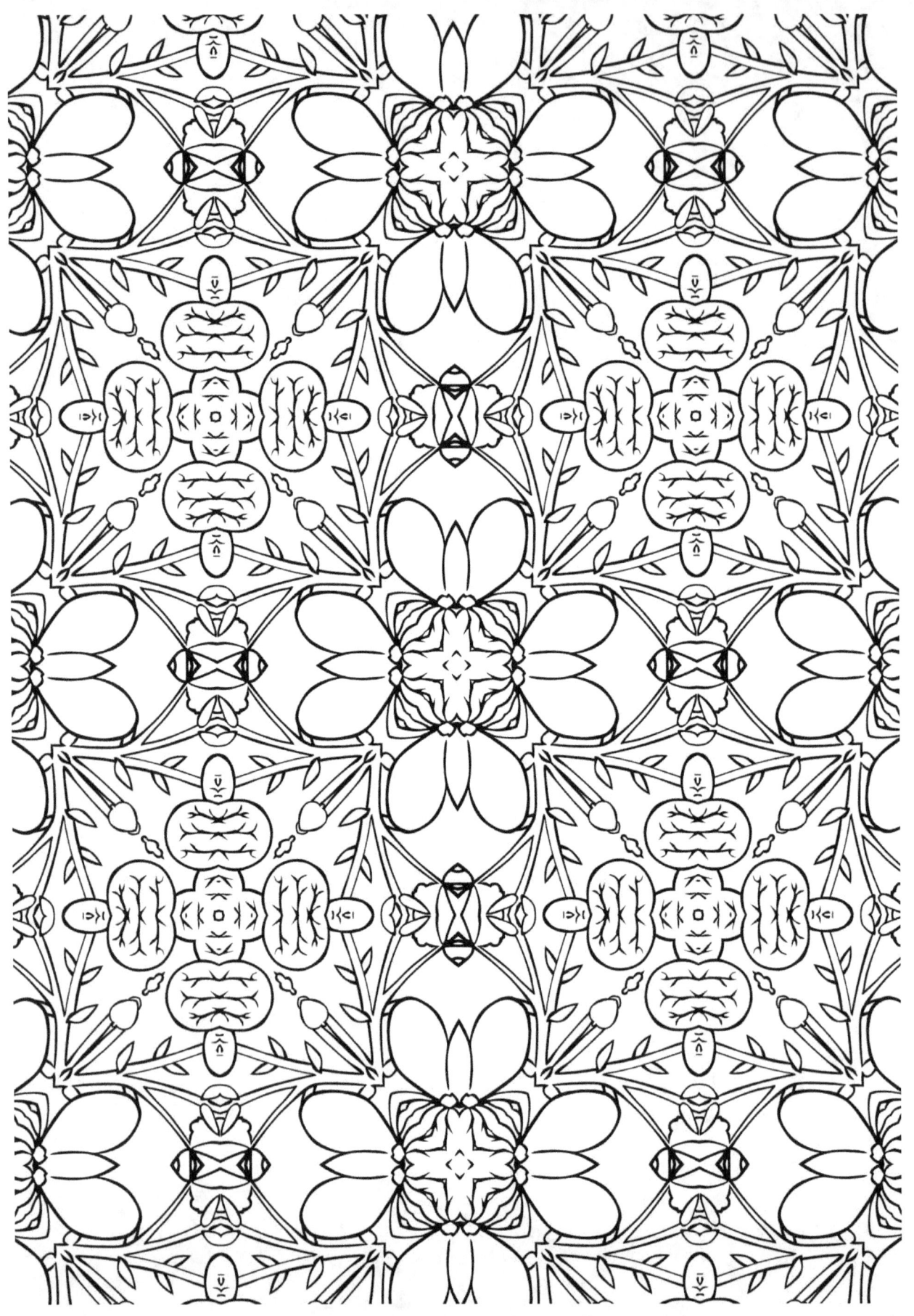

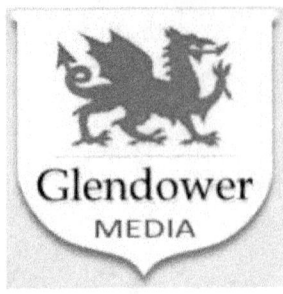

Find more fine books for coloring, humor, sports, music and art at our website www.glendowermedia.com.

Like us on Facebook

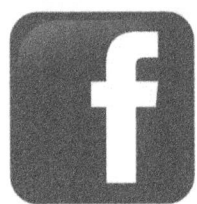

https://www.facebook.com/GlendowerMedia/